Your Amazing Itty Bitty Tax Audit Prevention Book

15 Essential Tips to Keep From Being Audited

In the eyes of the IRS, you are guilty until you prove yourself innocent. You must show that you reported all of your income. You must show that you spent the money for the allowable deductions you took on your tax return.

1. IRS uses a secret formula to select tax returns for audit.

2. Nobody knows what this formula is.

3. The formula scores your return compared to other returns in your industry, in your geographical area.

4. The higher the score, the higher your chance of winning the IRS audit lottery.

5. With the right planning, you CAN protect yourself.

In her ground breaking Itty Bitty Book, Enrolled Agent Nellie Williams teaches you not only how to avoid audits but what to do if you are audited.

If you buy one Itty Bitty Book this year, this may be the best investment you can make in yourself.

Your Amazing
Itty Bitty®

Tax Audit
Prevention Book

15 Essential Tips
to Keep From Being Audited

Nellie T. Williams, EA

Published by Itty Bitty® Publishing
A subsidiary of S & P Productions, Inc.

Copyright © 2015 Nellie T. Williams

Printed in the United States of America

Itty Bitty® Publishing
311 Main Street, Suite D
El Segundo, CA 90245
(310) 640-8885

ISBN: 978-1-931191-51-7

Thank you, IRS, for wanting to interview me. I didn't intend to take your job as Tax Auditor for the Internal Revenue Service. Now I can say I took that job by accident and it gave me a tremendous purpose and a great business:

> *"...to help YOU keep more of what's yours from becoming theirs - spelled THE-IRS!"* ©

Thank you, Dad, for believing in me.

Please visit our website to learn more about avoiding tax audits.

www.ittybittypublishing.com

or visit Nellie at

www.AuditProofYourTaxes.com

Table of Contents

Essential Tips

Tip 1
GUILTY!

In the eyes of the IRS, you are guilty until you prove yourself innocent. You must show that you reported all of your income. You must show that you spent the money for the allowable deductions you took on your tax return.

1. This is not Perry Mason.
2. You are not innocent until proven guilty.
3. Uncle Sam wants YOUR money.
4. Uncle Sam thinks you broke the tax laws.
5. Congress writes the tax laws.
6. IRS is the "tax police" that enforce the laws.
7. The job of the IRS auditor is to find your mistake.
8. The IRS is NOT your friend.
9. It is your job to prove you are right.
10. You don't have to be the Lone Ranger.
11. Tax professionals want to help you.

GUILTY!

- IRS is the only agency that can collect money for the government.
- IRS contacts you because they think you made an error on your return.
- It is YOUR job to show them your return is correct as you filed it.

Tip 2
Prevention: Mission Impossible!

The IRS decides which tax return it wants to examine or audit. You do not control the IRS. The only one you can control is yourself. You can help the IRS decide NOT to choose your return.

1. The IRS uses a secret formula to select tax returns for audit.
2. Nobody knows what this formula is.
3. The formula scores your return compared to other returns in your industry, in your geographical area.
4. The higher the score, the higher your chance of winning the IRS audit lottery.
5. With the right planning, you CAN protect yourself.
6. Avoiding an audit is not impossible.

Prevention: Mission Impossible!

- You cannot control the IRS.
- You CAN divert the IRS.
- You CAN play the tax game to win.
- Beat, not cheat, the IRS.
- Just report the truth, the whole truth and nothing but the truth.

Tip 3
What, Exactly, Is An IRS Audit?

The IRS will never begin their contact with you by email or by telephone. Anyone who tries to contact you that way is trying to scam you. The Internal Revenue Service will always begin their first contact with you by letter.

1. This letter will be mailed to your last known address.
2. File IRS Form 8822 to give the IRS your new address if you move.
3. An audit is a review of what you reported on your tax return.
4. The IRS will tell you what they want to look at.
5. Most audits today are by correspondence.
6. Some audits can be in person at the IRS.
7. Business audits are generally conducted at the business location.

What, Exactly, Is An IRS Audit?

- Written notice to appear with your records.
- Specific issues identified by IRS.
- A scary, nerve-rattling date with the auditor.
- Your chance to see how honest you really are.
- Your chance to see if you cheated yourself.

Tip 4
Can They Really Do That?

In a word, YES! It is the mission of the IRS to determine that the correct tax has been paid. They are charged by Congress to do their job. My job with the Internal Revenue Service was as an auditor in the Examination Division.

1. The auditor examines your tax return.
2. The auditor examines your books and records.
3. The auditor examines your receipts.
4. The auditor works in examination.
5. The collector works in collections.
6. The collector is a Revenue Officer.
7. The collector examines your financial situation.
8. The collector may offer you a payment plan.
9. The collector keeps track of your payments and reminds you if you are late.
10. Every IRS employee carries identification and credentials.
11. The Special Agent also carries a badge.
12. The Special Agent is truly like the tax police and can send you to tax jail.

Can They Really Do That?

- There are thousands of people who work for the government.
- Every employee has a job.
- Every employee has a personality.
- They can be nice.
- They do have authority and power.

Tip 5
How Can An Audit Turn Out For Me?

There are three basic results possible for your income tax audit.

1. IRS chose to audit your return because it showed a potential for error.
2. Is that error in YOUR favor?
3. It could be that the IRS owes YOU money.
4. That is called "Refund!"
5. Most of the time you can't prove what you claimed and YOU owe the IRS.
6. That is called "Balance Due."
7. Sometimes you can prove every penny you claimed and that means the IRS goes away empty-handed.
8. That is called "No-Change." :)
9. In any event, it is up to you.
10. It starts when you prepare your return.

How Can An Audit Turn Out For Me?

- Balance due the IRS = You pay IRS.
- Refund due the taxpayer = IRS pays you.
- No Change = You proved your position.
- No Change = You don't owe IRS money. :)
- No Change is rare, but it does happen.

Tip 6
What Can An Audit Really Cost Me?

Most people immediately answer this question with one word: Money. But an IRS audit can cost you more than money. Do you have to take time off work to appear at their office? Do you have to adjust work plans for them to come to your place of business?

1. An audit can cost you sleep.
2. An audit can cost you worry.
3. An audit can cost you health.
4. An audit can cost you business.
5. An audit can cost you focus.
6. An audit can cost you relationships.
7. An audit can cost you everything.
8. IRS statistics report the average 1040 audit results in $8,000 owed.
9. IRS statistics report the average business audit results in over $11,000 owed.
10. What will it cost you?

What Can An Audit Really Cost Me?

- You can lose your business.
- You can lose your business partner.
- You can lose your house.
- You can lose your spouse.
- You can lose your health.
- You can lose so much more than wealth.
- Do you have an extra $10K to pay?

Tip 7
Can They Audit More Than One Year?

Of course, the answer is YES. But there are rules in place to protect you, the taxpayer. The IRS is not usually examining a return the minute it is filed. Generally a year or two has gone by before a return is audited. Most of the time the auditor will want to look at the return for the year before.

1. IRS will examine your return.
2. If an adjustment or change is to be made, they will tell you.
3. If a similar change is in order for the year before, they will "open" that year for audit.
4. They may flag the next year's return to make sure you are not making the same mistake again.
5. If you proved everything the IRS was looking for in your first audit, and the next year is also chosen for audit of the same issue, you can use your "wild card" called Repetitive Audit Procedures to halt that second audit.
6. If the next year is chosen for different issues, the audit game is still on.
7. You must deal with the IRS.

Can They Audit More Than One Year?

- Owing money in year one may open year two.
- Proving an issue audited in year one protects same issue in the next year.
- New issue in the next year means audit is still on.
- Yes, IRS can go back in time, too.
- See Tips 12 and 13 for more information.

Tip 8
I Got A Notice. What Do I Do Now?

First, take a breath. I know your heart is racing. I know your stomach just turned upside down. Read the notice. Take your time. What do they want?

1. Every IRS Notice has a Notice Number.
2. Every notice is written in "legalese."
3. Look to see for WHAT YEAR they want more information.
4. Look to see WHAT ISSUES they want to verify.
5. Look to see by WHAT DATE they want you to respond.
6. Look for yourself to understand you can have someone represent you.
7. Not every notice is an audit notice.
8. Not every notice is correct.
9. If you think READ is a four letter word, this is one time it can help you!

I Got A Notice. What Do I Do Now?

- READ the notice.
- Identify the TAX YEAR.
- Identify the TAX ISSUES.
- Decide if you want to do this yourself, or
- Decide if you want professional help in the form of IRS Representation.

Tip 9
Who Are The Players In This Tax Game?

In the board game Monopoly, you roll the dice and move your playing piece around the board. Sometimes you land on Chance. Sometimes you land on Community Chest. Sometimes you do not pass "Go" but go directly to jail. Cast of Players:

1. The IRS computer scores your return.
2. The IRS auditor reviews your papers.
3. The IRS collector takes your money.
4. The IRS Special Agent carries a gold badge and can arrest you if you don't play nice.
5. The tax preparer is the person who prepared the tax return.
6. The tax professional is the person you engage to represent you in the audit experience.
7. The IRS Appeals Officer considers all appeals.
8. The tax attorney is the person who defends you in Tax Court if your case is that serious.
9. The Tax Court Judge is the arbiter of your case.

Who Are The Players In This Tax Game?

- IRS Auditor
- IRS Collector
- Tax Preparer
- You, the Taxpayer
- Your representative to help you
- You do not have to do this alone

Tip 10
And Now The State Wants "In?"

Most states in our country also have their own income tax laws and tax return forms. Most states' returns start with numbers and information from your completed federal tax return. So if there is a change to your federal return, there could also be a change to your state return.

1. The IRS and your state talk to each other.
2. It is totally normal for the state to join in.
3. If the IRS wants money as a result of your audit, the state probably wants some money too.
4. Your state could start their own audit without any prior federal audit.
5. Many states have been allowed to audit your federal return and then make changes to your state return, too.
6. The state audit usually begins some time (a few months to a year) after the federal audit is completed.
7. The person who helped you with your federal audit can help with your state audit, too.

And Now The State Wants "In?"

- READ the notice.
- Identify the TAX YEAR.
- Identify the TAX ISSUES.
- Decide if you want to do this yourself, or
- Decide if you want professional help in the form of State representation.
- If you had someone help you with a federal audit, you may want them to help with your state audit, too.

Tip 11
Can I Appeal?

Yes. At almost any time in the audit process you can appeal the findings or determination of the auditor. EVERY employee has a boss, or supervisor. All you have to do is ask.

1. During the audit process, you can ask to speak to the auditor's supervisor.
2. After the audit report is rendered, you can request to go to the Appeals Division.
3. The Appeals Division is separate from the Audit Division.
4. The main objective of Appeals is to settle your case before you take it to Tax Court.
5. Going to Tax Court is your right, but is very costly.

Can I Appeal?

- Yes, but you must ASK to speak to someone else.
- The job of the auditor is to determine that the correct amount of tax was paid.
- Sometimes a misunderstanding can be cleared up by talking with a supervisor.
- The job of the Appeals Officer is to try to settle your case to keep it out of Tax Court.
- The Tax Court calendar is very crowded.

Tip 12
How Far Back Can The IRS Go?

It's bad enough you have to prove last year's tax return. IRS is almost always working on prior years' returns. Examining current returns as they are filed is often limited to correcting processing errors or stopping identified fraud schemes.

1. IRS usually only examines, or audits, "open" returns.
2. A return is considered "open" based on the statute of limitations. (Next tip)
3. If an error is identified in one open year, IRS can go back to an earlier open year if they think the same error was made.
4. If the audit issue involves something that allowed a loss to be carried back to an earlier year, that earlier year can be opened for examination of that issue.
5. Usually IRS will only go back 3 years.
6. IRS can go back 7 years if you omit income.
7. IRS can go back FOREVER if you commit tax fraud.
8. Always keep a copy of your tax returns.

How Far Back Can The IRS Go?

- IRS usually only goes back 3 years.
- IRS can go back 7 years if you omit income.
- IRS WILL go back FOREVER if you commit tax fraud.
- ALWAYS keep your copies of your tax returns FOREVER.
- You never know when you need your copy for your own protection.

Tip 13
What is this "Statute of Limitations"?

The IRS is governed by the tax laws enacted by the US Congress. Tax laws are always changing. But the statute (law) of limitations governs the time IRS has to do their work. Each IRS Division has their own time frame.

1. By federal law, your IRS tax return is open for examination for 3 years from the due date of the return or the date it was filed, whichever is later.
2. By state law, your STATE tax return is open for at least one more year.
3. Some states have two additional years according to their state's laws.
4. Once the clock runs out on the time to examine, or the time to collect the tax, the statute is "blown."
5. You can allow the IRS more time by extending the statute on a specific year.
6. Sometimes it is in your best interest to extend the statute.
7. Sometimes it is in your best interest to allow the statute to expire.

What Is This "Statute of Limitations"?

- A 1040 tax return filed on 4-15-15 is open for audit for 3 years, until 4-15-18.
- A 1040 tax return filed on 2-15-15 is open for audit for 3 years, until 4-15-18.
- A 1040 return filed on 6-15-15 is open for audit for 3 years until 6-15-18.
- Your state could add one or two more years.
- When in doubt, consult your tax advisor.

Tip 14
How can I best protect myself?

The IRS selects your return because they think they will find a mistake and they might be able to collect more money from you. How do you prove yourself innocent when they think you are guilty? Documentation. Paperwork. Receipts.

1. Keep your tax returns forever. Period.
2. Keep your receipts for the current year for at least five years (or seven for CA).
3. 2014 taxes filed in 2015, plus four years, totals five years for most states. (6 more for California = 7 years.)
4. Keep paperwork for assets you own until 5 years (7 for CA) after you sell the asset.
5. You've heard "a man who represents himself has a fool for a client."
6. Seek professional advice. Allow a tax professional to help you.
7. Understand that "when in doubt, throw it out" is the mantra of the IRS auditor.
8. In other words, if you decide you don't want to follow the rules for proving deductions or expenses – then also decide not to claim them on your tax return.

How Can I Best Protect Myself?

- Would you give yourself a root canal?
- Get help for your tax audit, too.
- Keep your tax returns forever.
- Keep your tax receipts as long as they matter.
- Consult with a professional who can advise you on how long those receipts can matter.
- Invest in tax audit help to save you money and heartache in the long run.
- Realize the IRS is your silent partner when it comes to filing your tax return.
- Do all you can do to protect yourself, your business, your family and your money.
- When it is time to destroy your paperwork, use a cross-cut shredder.

Tip 15
Where can I get help?

Just like in any industry or profession, there are good guys and bad buys, better guys and best guys. When looking for assistance, ask your friends, ask for referrals or recommendations, check credentials. Below are some resources.

1. IRS.gov for you do-it-yourselfers.
2. NAEA.org. Find an EA at the National Association of Enrolled Agents.
3. NATPTax.com. Find a Tax Preparer at the National Association of Tax Professionals.
4. NSACCT.org. Find a Professional at the National Society of Accountants.
5. AuditProofYourTaxes.com. Connect with Nellie T Williams, EA, The IRS Insider. Find out how her Audit Proofing System can help you, even before you need it.

Where Can I Get Help?

- Check the websites mentioned.
- Ask your friends who they trust
- Ask your own preparer for help.
- Consult AuditProofYourTaxes.com for this author's IRS Insider Information and Audit Proofing System.

You've finished. Before you go...

Tweet/share that you finished this book.
Please star rate this book in the site
where you purchased it.

Reviews are solid gold to writers. Please
take a few minutes to give us some itty
bitty feedback on this book.

ABOUT THE AUTHOR

No little girl dreams of being an auditor when she grows up. Neither did Nellie. She grew up in Lake Bluff, Illinois, heralded by the Chicago Tribune as the most patriotic little town in America. The Fourth of July is her most favorite holiday next to Christmas.

She moved to Phoenix, Arizona, with her family and loves their two seasons: hot and hotter. :) Even during tax season, she loves to sing in her church choir at Gloria Dei Lutheran Church in Paradise Valley, Arizona.

Nellie is often asked, "Are you still an agent for the IRS?" No, after leaving the IRS, Nellie became an Enrolled Agent. An EA is enrolled with the Department of the Treasury to act as YOUR agent at all levels of the IRS anywhere in the world they have an office.

AuditProofYourTaxes.com is a division of Williams Audit Specialists of Arizona, Inc. Because she is limited in how many people she can help one-on-one at her desk during tax season, she developed her training program to help more people. She has been teaching for over 30 years and invites you to learn how you, too, can pay your fair share and not a penny more.

Nellie is blessed to be married to her husband, Steve, who totally supports her in her business.

Other Amazing Itty Bitty® Books

- **Your Amazing Itty Bitty® Business Tax Book** – Deborah A. Morgan, CAP

- **Your Amazing Itty Bitty® Book of QuickBooks® Shortcuts** - Barbara L. Starley, CPA

- **Your Amazing Itty Bitty® Personal Bookkeeping Book** - Joe DiChiara, CPA
-
With many more Amazing Itty Bitty® Books available on line….